Copyright © 2020 Victoria J.Brown & Pos
The right of Victoria J.Brown & Positivity Pants Prints to
Work has been asserted by them in accordance Copyri[g]
Apart from any use permitted under UK copyright la[w]
reproduced, stored, or transmitted, any form, or by an[y]
writing of the publisher, Victoria J.Brown & Positivity [P]
reprographic production, in accordance with the terms of licences issued by the Copyright
Licensing Agency.

The information given in this book should not be treated as a substitute for professional medical advice. If you feel you have symptoms that require professional medical advice, always see a medical practitioner. Any use of the information in this book is at the reader's discretion. The author and the publisher cannot be held responsible for any loss, claim or damage arising from the use, or misuse, of the suggestions made, the failure to take medical advice or for any material from Victoria J.Brown or third party websites.

*It takes 21 days to create a habit ...
& 90 days to create a lifestyle ...*

Welcome, welcome, welcome to **'21 days of putting on your positivity pants'**.

A huge thank you for being here & a huge well done on wanting to live a more positive, happy & peaceful life.

This isn't 'any old journal' ... the advice in this book has been my own 'go to' when things haven't been as great as they could be.

Throughout this journal you will see snippets of my story and how coming from a place of gratitude, positivity and love can truly help you to live a high vibe life.

So, I hope you make the most of the exercises, the journaling and the colouring ... (and just to say, yes, I'm based in the U.K, but the U.S version of 'journaling' looks so much better to me than our U.K 'Journalling' ... don't you think? 😊

And, because with any kind of positive pants you are wearing, we get to do what is best for us ... so 'journaling' it will be ☺ feel free to change it as you go along ... hey, it's your journal 😊

So, before the writer in me digresses, let me introduce myself ...

I'm **Vic Brown, a.k.a, 'Positivity Queen'** (a name given by my family, friends & even clients ...yes, I love it too!☺)

I'm an Author, who is certified in The Law of Attraction, I hold a Masters in Creative Writing & I'm a Journaling Addict!

I was journaling before I even knew it was 'a thing'. It's been my go-to since I could write. As I've grown, journaling has helped me in so many ways and once you discover how it can soothe your soul, lift your spirits and bring to you the life you deserve, you'll be filling notebooks and ⭐ manifesting your desires like the magical being you are supposed to be.

Journaling can help anyone live a high vibe life because you 'get to' understand your emotions rather than brushing them under the carpet, ignoring them and the worst burying them deep!

Journaling allows you to explore and come out the other side so YOU CAN LIVE THE WONDERFUL LIFE YOU DESERVE 🖤

You can see the links below so you can have an abundance of positivity thrown your way.

When we come from a place of love & positivity, our world can change drastically. However, if we're not surrounded by high-vibes, it can be hard to attract & manifest that positive happy life we so desire.

If you'd like to follow the positive pants vibes 🩲 I'd love for you to follow 'me' and 'positive pants prints' on our 'social media' routes ... you can see them below!

One last thing ... I know life is busy, but take 10 minutes to feel into this process every single day and watch the changes that happen within your life.

Come and get some positive pants high vibes with us ...

- 📷 /victoriaj.brown
- 📷 /positivepantsprints
- 📘 /vicjbrown
- 📘 positive pants FB group https://bit.ly/3wBGy1E
- 🐦 @victoriajbrown

Please visit teachable for the courses available:
https://victoriajbrown.teachable.com/

Visit the positive pants prints shop - **www.victoria-brown.com**

> Positive thinking is a habit, like everything else, you get better at it with time
>
> Alexander Gustafsson

Why 21 days of putting on your positivity pants?

You have probably heard the phrase, '
It takes 21 days to break a habit'.

Did you realise this quote has been changed over the years?

Maxwell Maltz, a plastic surgeon from the 1950/60's, quoted, in his book, **Psycho Cybernetics**, 'These, and many other commonly observed phenomena tend to show that it requires a minimum of 21 days for an old mental image to dissolve and a new one to jell'.

Maltz would perform operations, such as giving a patient a new nose, and he found it would take at least 21 days for the patient to get used to their new look. It was the same with patients who had a limb amputated. He found it took around 21 days before the patient would adjust to the feeling. They would experience phantom feelings that their arm or leg was still there. It was this that led to Maltz looking into behaviours, and he noticed it took himself at least 21 days to form a new habit.

Over the decades his quote lost the word 'minimum', and is now the well-known phrase,
'It takes 21 days to break a habit'.

The problem with such a bold statement is that everyone is different, so something one person may find easy to adapt to, may seem horrendously hard for the next person.

'Having a positive mindset is also a habit,
just as negative thinking is a habit.
How you automatically respond
to something becomes a habit.'
- Gandhi -

However, if you have any habits you would like to change or any new habits you'd like to bring into your life, it starts with mindset.

Having a positive mindset is the key to staying focused when it comes to developing new habits.

Wouldn't it be fab to get into the habit of only putting on your positivity pants? No other clothing to choose from, except a drawer full of positivity pants only.

This journal aims to give you a 21-day kick-start, of getting up every morning and putting on your positive pants. As I've mentioned, 21 days isn't a 'fit all' statistic, but the idea is to get you started. Make it a habit of wanting to be inspired and want to inspire others. It will hopefully help you get into a routine of choosing to put on your positive pants daily.

In the words of, **Zig Ziglar**,
'People often say that motivation doesn't last.
Well, neither does bathing that's why we recommend it daily.'

Although this book is 21 days of wearing your positivity pants, you may think I'm leaving you naked after and stripping you of those pants after 21 days ... I'm not! I promise!

Make sure you connect with us on our social media platforms, so we can keep you in the positive pants frame of mind!

Do not stop wearing your positive pants, I want you to keep putting them on every single day.

You can find more positivity power on my website
www.victoria-brown.com

The key to this book is to get you into the habit of wearing your positivity pants only. Give your drawers a clear out, bin all those negative knickers, boring boxers and turbulent trunks, there's no room for them in our positivity pants drawer.

YOU'VE GOT THIS

21 days of a positive pants mindset will hopefully give you the incentive to wear your positivity pants every day forever! Yes, guys, that's the aim.

This is a little encouragement to show you that wearing your positive pants can be so much fun.

In life, you can't control some situations or circumstances and you most definitely can't control other people. Not everyone will do as you would do. However, you can choose how you respond. When you choose to wear your positive pants, you'll always be a winner.

Proudly wear those positive pants & spread the love guys

Love, Light & Hugs
Vic
xxx

How to use this journal?

Every day take time out to read the 'positive pants of the day', breathe through any exercises and journal your thoughts.

If you have the 'positive pants ; the notebook' too, use this to express your thoughts more clearly if needed, (or course, use your own notebook if not).

Work through the questions, FEEL into your answers. This is the key to making this work; the FEELING! We often brush over things, rush through life and we don't stop to take in our journey.

I've put this journal together with complete love, joy and happiness so that you stop and take in the beauty of your life, see the positives and FEEL into this. You will see the word 'FEEL', capitalised as a reminder for you to do just that; FEEL THE FEELING 🖤

Each day has been put together with kindness in hope that it will help you see your own worth so that you can live the life you deserve.

You can use this journal at whatever time of the day suits you, I would recommend on a morning because it will help to give you some energy and spark for the day ahead ... but you may have young children who will interrupt this moment (been there) or you may work shifts, so mornings don't work for you. Just allow yourself the time to breathe through the exercises and journaling, so you can get the most out of each day.

Some of the journaling exercises are created for you to come back to, so that you can think about the questions being asked and truly FEEL into your answers.

Each day also has a colouring therapy quote allowing you to feel into the words on the page as you brighten up the picture ... take time out to FEEL into these too.

Now, there's ONE RULE ... HAVE FUN
SIMPLY ENJOY PUTTING ON YOU POSITIVE PANTS EVERY SINGLE DAY!

NOTES

CHOOSE POSITIVE PANTS 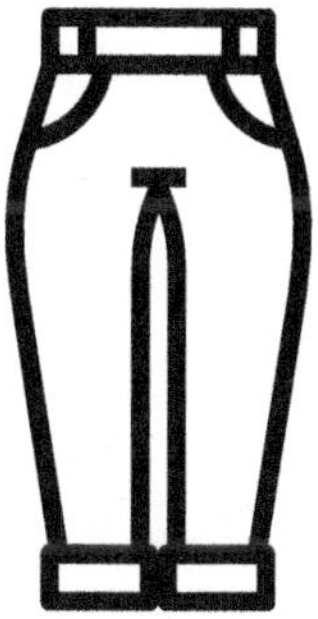 DAILY, AS THEY FEEL BETTER  THAN  WEARING ANY OTHER PANTS

NOTES

DAY ONE
GRATITUDE
POSITIVITY PANTS

'Gratitude is a powerful catalyst for happiness. It's the spark that lights a fire of joy in your soul'
- Amy Collette -

Gratitude is the core of having a positive mindset.

Once you start looking at things to appreciate in your life,
you'll have more to appreciate.

The Law of Attraction shows that if we concentrate on the
positive or negative aspects of our life, we bring more of that to us.
(It is deeper than this and there is more too it, but this book is to help you get your
positive pants on, not to delve into every aspect of the Universe, this is a little part
of it and I'm sure if you sit and think about it, it makes sense).

Therefore, focus on things you are grateful for,
and you'll have more to be thankful for.

Write down 3 things you are grateful for at this moment in time ...

_____

_____

_____

_____

_____

_____

_____

> 'Be thankful for what you have; you'll end up having more. If you concentrate on what you don't have, you will never, ever have enough.'
> — Oprah Winfrey —

In my younger days, before I discovered the Law of Attraction and qualified as a practitioner, I had a very negative mindset.

Nothing ever went my way. Everything was a hassle. I hated my job. I was always seeking more ... and guess what, all I attracted to me was more misery. I constantly whinged about what was NOT right in my life. If someone had said to me, 'Think of all the things you have to be grateful for,' I'd have laughed and said, 'Like what?' *CRINGE*

I was too focused on what other people had, focused on where I wanted to be in life, focused on everything being hard work ... and guess what ... yes, you've guessed it, IT WAS!

Over the years, it got worse and worse and worse ... so I constantly focused on the 'worst'. It was in these darkest days when I was unsure of how we could climb out of the hole when I discovered the Law of Attraction. When I felt things couldn't get ANY worse! (This is a novel in itself ... so I won't digress too much!)

It was in these days I started looking at things I had to be grateful for ... it wasn't long before things started to turn around AND it wasn't long before this way of thinking became addictive, until it became natural (and YES, journaling most definitely helped!).

Go back to the 3 things you are grateful for and write down WHY you are grateful for them & how they make you FEEL ...

_____

_____

_____

_____

_____

_____

_____

**One of the best ways to start appreciating life
is to write a gratitude list.**

Okay, so we started with 3 things ... but let's really challenge you!

Write 100 things you are grateful for!

100? REALLY?

This exercise will make you feel amazing!

It can include things that you may take for granted, such as, clean water, hot water, electricity, a roof over your head, clothes to wear, food, family, friends ...

... so dig deep when you write this list.

Once you have written this list, keep it close as a reminder of all the things you have in your life that should be appreciated.

A great way to end your day is to write down all the good things about your day, all the things that you appreciated about that day.

Once you get into the habit of coming from a place of gratitude, you'll soon find you have more to appreciate.

*'The world becomes a brighter
and happier place when you
come from a place of gratitude &
show appreciation to yourself & to others'*

So let's do this ... sit somewhere comfortable and quiet so you can breathe gently into your space and truly think about all the things you are grateful for ...

1. _____
2. _____
3. _____
4. _____
5. _____
6. _____
7. _____
8. _____
9. _____
10. _____
11. _____
12. _____
13. _____
14. _____
15. _____
16. _____
17. _____
18. _____
19. _____
20. _____
21. _____
22. _____
23. _____
24. _____
25. _____
26. _____
27. _____
28. _____
29. _____
30. _____
31. _____
32. _____
33. _____
34. _____
35. _____
36. _____
37. _____
38. _____
39. _____
40. _____

41.
42.
43.
44.
45.
46.
47.
48.
49.
50.
51.
52.
53.
54.
55.
56.
57.
58.
59.
60.
61.
62.
63.
64.
65.
66.
67.
68.
69.
70.
71.
72.
73.
74.
75.
76.
77.
78.
79.
80.

81. _____
82. _____
83. _____
84. _____
85. _____
86. _____
87. _____
88. _____
89. _____
90. _____
91. _____
92. _____
93. _____
94. _____
95. _____
96. _____
97. _____
98. _____
99. _____
100. _____

One more task for today ...
How did writing that list make you FEEL?

_____
_____
_____
_____
_____
_____
_____
_____
_____
_____

NOTES

NOTES

DAY 2
DECLUTTERING
POSITIVITY PANTS

'When we throw out the
physical clutter, we clear our
minds. When we throw out
the mental clutter,
we clear our souls'
- Gail Blanke -

When we talk about decluttering, we generally think about the physical 'stuff' in our homes or office space ... and to be fair, plenty of research has been conducted to show that clutter can affect the mind. If papers, knick-knacks or mess surround you, it can affect your ability to focus on certain tasks.

So today, let's focus on decluttering any physical 'stuff' that needs to be removed from your personal space.

If you can't do this today, try and schedule it in for a few days time.

Don't think of this as an option: this is a MUST. This is something that HAS to be done. Think of it as a doctor's appointment or a work meeting ... something that you wouldn't cancel. This decluttering is a job that NEEDS doing.

It could be one or a few rooms in your house, a wardrobe of clothes that needs emptying, a pile of bills/papers that need filing; anything that you know will make you feel better.

Something that is niggling at the back of your mind that you keep putting off because you don't have time. This is the time to do it. Get it scheduled in your diary. I'd advise you do it within the 21 days, sooner rather than later, because it will help the rest of your positive pants journey.

Sit for a moment and write about how the above task makes you FEEL? What emotions are coming up for you here?

_____
_____
_____
_____
_____
_____
_____

> 'Clutter is not just physical stuff.
> It's old ideas, toxic relationships and
> bad habits. Clutter is anything that
> does not support your better self.'
> - Eleanor Brownn -

Over the next couple of pages plan your decluttering time ... now as Eleanor Brownn said, this doesn't have to be physical stuff, maybe something is holding you back from fulfilling the life you truly desire. So, truly think into this when you're planning your decluttering session.

> 'Cleaning clutter releases huge amounts of
> energy in the body. When you get rid of
> everything in your life that has no real
> meaning or significance for you.
> You literally feel lighter in
> body, mind & spirit'
> - Karen Kingston -

How does the above quote by Karen Kingston make you FEEL?

_____
_____
_____
_____
_____
_____
_____
_____

You may find some resistance against doing this decluttering task, excuses such as, 'not enough time', 'it's not a priority' or even fear may play a part if you are removing yourself from a toxic environment.

BUT ... Trust me when I say this will rocket you forward because you'll feel as if a weight has been lifted.

Below write a plan that focuses on a decluttering session; When? What room/activity? Who will help? And any other important planning that is needed for this task ...

_____
_____
_____
_____
_____
_____
_____
_____
_____
_____
_____
_____
_____
_____
_____
_____
_____
_____
_____
_____
_____
_____

What reward will you give yourself?

What reward you may ask! YES!

When we complete tasks that are on our 'to-do' list having a reward at the end can truly entice us to finish the task at hand.

_____
_____
_____
_____
_____
_____
_____
_____

Imagine you've completed the task of decluttering, how would you FEEL? Feeling into the peace can be just as fulfilling as any reward.

_____
_____
_____
_____
_____
_____
_____
_____

**Keep imagining that FEELING
when you feel you are losing motivation.
This will keep you going when the task feels too big!**

NOTES

NOTES

DAY 3
NON-JUDGY
POSITIVITY PANTS

'If I stop judging other people,
I free myself from
being judged and
I can dance.'
- Patti Digh -

Okay, let's jump straight in with some journaling ...

Do you have family and friends that you criticise?
_____
_____
_____

Do you find yourself analysing their lives and telling yourself, you wouldn't do that? Or, you'd do something better?
_____
_____
_____

Do you have an opinion on how others live their lives?
_____
_____
_____

Do you criticise yourself?
_____
_____
_____

How does all the above make you FEEL?
_____
_____
_____
_____
_____
_____

Today, we are putting on those non-judgy positive pants.

It's important to remember we are all different. And wouldn't it be a boring world if we were all the same?

Judging of others, or yourself stops the appreciation game. You can't come from a place of gratitude if you are judging.

> 'Judging is preventing us from understanding a new truth.
> Free yourself from the rules of old judgements and create the space for new understanding'
> - Steve Maraboli -

Today, recognise how much judging you do.

Think of someone you judge: it could be that you don't agree with their actions, you don't like a particular behaviour, it could even come down to judging their clothes ...

How does the above statement affect you?

_____
_____
_____

One of the biggest things people do is judge themselves ...

Do you judge yourself? How can you improve this?

_____
_____
_____

> 'Your best changes from moment to moment,
> sick or well, tired or rested.
> Remember that you are
> an imperfect human being.
> There is no value to judging yourself'
> - Miguel Angel Ruiz -

Today, we are going to STOP with the judgy pants.

You could be thinking, 'How?' 'They annoy me,' 'They've hurt me,' 'They've made me angry,' etc.

The best way to put your judgy pants in the bin and replace them with non-judgy pants is to write down everything you LOVE about this person, including yourself if you feel you judge yourself more than others. The latter is such a common occurrence, if this is the case for you, definitely start with YOU first.

Write down all the things you LOVE about yourself.

Write from your heart and don't let your mind/ego interfere. I can give you your first wonderful attribute; I LOVE that you are using this book and you are open to putting on your positive pants daily. This is truly awesome.

You are truly awesome!

_____
_____
_____
_____
_____
_____
_____

Now let's look at someone whom you may judge more than you'd like to ...

It's important to remember you can't change people, and neither should you want to, just as no one should try to change you.

Sometimes, we don't like a personality trait in someone and often this reflects something about ourselves that we don't like. We usually don't realise this, because we don't want to admit it to ourselves.

You will have attracted this person into your life because there is something that you love about them; something that reflects your personality and character.

Sometimes people come into our lives for a lifetime, or a season, but always for a reason!

Use below to write about the positive effects this person has had on your life and why you are grateful they have been present in your world ...

_____
_____
_____
_____
_____
_____
_____
_____

Can you feel the difference when you come from a place of love & gratitude?

Try to remember this when those negative judgy thoughts start to arise, squash them with a positive thought so you can live a lighter more positive life.

NOTES

NOTES

DAY 4
FORGIVENESS
POSITIVITY PANTS

'Forgiveness is not always easy.
At times, it feels more painful
than the wound we suffered,
to forgive the one that
inflicted it. And yet, there is no
peace without forgiveness'
- Marianne Williamson -

Yesterday, we talked about putting on our non-judgy pants, so it seems natural to follow that with putting on our forgiveness pants.

> *'It's one of the greatest gifts you can give yourself, to forgive. Forgive everybody'*
> *- Maya Angelou -*

The only person who gets hurt when it comes to forgiveness is the person unwilling to forgive. Bitterness eats away at a person's soul and this is unhealthy for the mind and body.

If we go from the exercise yesterday, where we replaced judgement with love. Today, we are taking that one step further and adding forgiveness. Forgiveness doesn't mean you have to allow people back into your life, it doesn't mean you're willing to be walked over, **but it does mean you can move on.**

To let **IT** go, whatever **IT** is, is the healthiest way to live.

How does all of the above make you FEEL? What does this bring up for you?

_____
_____
_____
_____
_____
_____
_____

Maybe you need to work on forgiving yourself for an incident that has happened, or perhaps you haven't been kind to yourself, it's time to move on and forgive yourself.

You may not agree with the way a person treated you, or behaved towards another person but while you hold onto that lack of forgiveness you are blocking the opportunity for a fun-filled life.

If someone chooses not to be in your life, if someone hurts you, if someone acts in a way that you don't agree with, you have to understand that this is their choice and this will impact their life, but don't let it influence yours.

You can choose the way you respond to it.

Today, we are choosing our forgiveness positivity pants.

In this next exercise you can use your imagination ...

Put yourself in the other person's shoes and imagine 'you are them' and write down how you would feel in their position ...

If it's yourself you need to forgive, try to imagine you are someone who loves you, what do you want them to see ...

_____
_____
_____
_____
_____
_____
_____
_____

'To forgive is to set a prisoner free and discover that the prisoner was you'
- Lewis B. Smedes -

Now with this in mind, similar to the exercise you did yesterday, focus on the person that you choose to forgive (yes, even yourself) and write about all the things you love about this person.

_____
_____
_____
_____
_____
_____
_____
_____
_____
_____

Focus on replacing anguish, hurt and bitterness with love, warmth and understanding.

Choose to bring peace to your soul.

Remember, you can't choose other people's responses, you can only choose your own.

NOTES

DAY 5
KINDNESS
POSITIVITY PANTS

'No act of kindness,
no matter how small,
is ever wasted'
- Aesop -

Hopefully, by today, you are in a forgiving and non-judgy place. Hopefully, you are coming from a place of compassion for yourself and others. Once you are attuned to releasing judgement and forgiveness, you'll understand kindness.

> 'Be kind to unkind people.
> They need it the most.'
> - Ashleigh Brilliant -

How does the above make you FEEL?

_____
_____
_____
_____

Everybody needs a bit of kindness. A smile, a compliment or offering a helping hand can make someone's day.

You may feel someone isn't kind to you, but as we discussed yesterday, you choose your response.

If you feel someone isn't kind to you, or to others, they more than likely need you to open your heart to them. People who are happy with themselves can be unkind to others as it's a subconscious way of releasing their own self-loathing.

It's important to understand that someone else's actions and behaviour is a reflection of THEM! Just as your response to their actions and behaviour is a reflection of YOU!

People who are happy want to spread that happiness. They want others to feel the happy, positive vibes they feel.

It makes them happy to be around happy people ... this makes sense right?

They feed off high vibes, fun, laughter & positivity ... they feed off it as much as they spread it.

It's these people who get up every morning and put on their positivity pants. How do you FEEL about being that person?

_____

_____

_____

_____

Sometimes, it's not that people are unkind, it's that they forget to be kind.

People become wrapped up in their own lives, they forget to put on their positivity pants and they forget to spread the love.

Often, when we are out and about, in a world of our own (to-do lists, schedules, what should we have for dinner, which child needs what for school etc.) and unless something stops us in our steps and disrupts our thoughts, we forget to appreciate the moments and the little things.

When was the last time you walked into a shop and smiled at the people you passed? Or even drummed up a little conversation?

Now, don't get me wrong, there will be days where you simply can't be bothered to talk to anyone, however, we are on the positivity pants journey, so not being bothered isn't an option! This sounds harsh, I don't mean it to, I just want you to think of this as a no alternative mission; to wear positive pants because there are no others to wear.

Once you realise there is no other option but to smile & be kind, you will naturally want to be kind. You will naturally smile, nod and laugh with people all day long.

A quick nod at a stranger, a smile at the parent whose child is playing up or holding the door for someone, could make his or her day. We don't know what is going on in other people's lives, we often don't realise that a small, simple kind gesture could have the most significant impact on another's day, week or month.

When was the last time you did something kind for someone?

_____

_____

_____

Do you know, even a simple text to a friend to say you're thinking about them, will not only make THEM FEEL good, but it will also make YOU FEEL good too.

We often become wrapped up in our own busy lives, we forget to check in on those that we care about.

> 'Too often we underestimate the power of a touch, a smile, a kind word, a listening ear, an honest compliment or the smallest act of caring, all of which have the potential to turn a life around.'
> — Leo Buscaglia —

Your task today is to perform 5 acts of kindness. Yes, not 1 or 2 acts ... but 5 acts.

If you can do more, that would be awesome! Come back and write down your acts of kindness here, continue on the notes pages if needed ...

1. _____
2. _____
3. _____
4. _____
5. _____

Doesn't that feel great? The aim is to keep being kind until it becomes a natural part of you.

NOTES

DAY 6
GENEROSITY
POSITIVITY PANT

'A pessimist, they say, sees a glass as being half-empty; An optimist sees the same glass as half-full. But a giving person sees a glass of water and starts looking for someone who might be thirsty'
- G. Donald Gale -

By day six you should be brimming with forgiveness, non-judgement, handing out your kindness pants and being genuinely grateful for life.

Hopefully, you are feeling it. But remember, it's only Day 6, but it's important to be getting up every morning and pulling on those positive pants. You'll see how your positive pants collection will all come together as the days go on.

Are you feeling it? If so, express your feelings here. If not, what can you do today to FEEL into the above?

_____
_____
_____
_____
_____
_____
_____
_____
_____
_____
_____
_____

> 'True generosity is an offering,
> given freely and out of pure love.
> No strings attached. No expectations.
> Time and love are the most valuable
> possession you can share'
> - Suze Orman -

You see, everything is interlinked; when you have those positive pants on (whichever positive pants you decide to wear) your vibrations are high, so you'll want to spread the love.

**And as it all comes together
you will find yourself wanting to give.**

Now, one of the most precious things you can give is your time.

Being generous isn't about giving presents or money; it's about giving from your heart. Offering your time, expertise, a listening ear are some of the ways in which you can be wearing those generosity pants.

Offer someone your time today. Do something for someone that will make his or her day better. For example, walking someone's dog, helping someone with their shopping or just giving your time over a cup of tea to listen to someone.

When you've done this today, make a note of it here. How did it make you FEEL?

_____
_____
_____
_____
_____
_____
_____
_____
_____

**Get those generosity pants on and
feel the positivity shine from you.**

NOTES

NOTES

DAY 7
POSITIVE WORDS PANTS

'Positive messages throughout the day, keep the negative thoughts away.' says, 'ME!'

You've probably heard the saying 'sticks & stones may break my bones but names will never hurt me' ... sound familiar right?

I think it's fair to say the above is not true!

Words have the power to energise or bring you down. They have the power to influence your mind in more ways than you may realise.

We all know how much the online world has allowed our words to travel even further. How online bullying has enabled mean words to hit hard from only one or two words, let alone sentences!

The impact of negative or positive words can truly affect our day, hell, it can affect our world.

I won't digress too much in this journal, however, it is important for our positive pants exercises to **understand the power of your words and especially the words you speak to yourself!**

This latter point is **key to how we think and feel about ourselves**, and how this vibration can extend beyond us and impact the people and things around us.

So for today ...

Your challenge and mantra is to:

'USE POSITIVE WORDS ONLY'

How do you FEEL about using only high vibe words all day, every day?

_____
_____
_____
_____
_____
_____
_____

> 'Words can inspire.
> And words can destroy.
> Choose yours well'
> - Robin Sharma -

The 'use positive words only', works even better if you can get others to join in.

Can you encourage your colleagues at work, or your family and friends to join you? The more positive words used, the higher the positive energies will surround you all.

Say things, such as, 'Good Vibes Only'.

If you can shout the words, this will lift your mood and vibrations even higher.

Imagine sitting in an office and having a positive words game, where every 5 minutes someone has to shout out something positive.

If you don't work in that type of environment, don't be afraid to shout out those positive words when you're alone.

The universe is listening and wants to encourage you to keep those positive pants on. So just let go and release all those pent-up positive words.

On the following page you'll find a positive word game ... fill in the blanks, it will help you connect with the word.

Use these words and some of your own positive words; create sentences, have fun, sing the words, shout them ... Do what you can to truly FEEL the positivity.

If you think you are going to say something negative, STOP! Replace the word with a positive one.

HAVE FUN!

POSITIVE WORD GAME

FILL IN THE BLANKS AND THEN USE THESE WORDS THROUGHOUT THE DAY
(ANSWERS AT THE BOTTOM)

1. L _ V _   2. _ L _ VE   3. H _ G   4. DI _ I _ E

5. ZI _ _   6. B _ B _ LY   7. M _ T _ VAT _   8. J _ Y

9. W _ ND _ R _ UL   10. MAN _ F _ ST   11. B _ IG _ T

12. SH _ _ E   13. _ NE _ GY   14. EFF _ _ VE _ CE _ T

15. _ EAC _   16. _ WE _ OME

17. EN _ H _ S _ AST _ C   18. H _ A _ ING

19. B _ LIE _ E   20. _ OU _ AGE _ US   21. V _ B _ _ NT

22. _ EL _ GH _   23. EX _ U _ S _ TE   24. R _ LA _

25. MA _ V _ L _ OU _   26. TH _ IV _ NG   27. C _ LM

28. _ AU _ HT _ R.   29. V _ SU _ L _ SA _ IO _

30. E _ C _ UR _ GE   31. A _ AZ _ NG   32. H _ RM _ NY

33. GR _ TIT _ _ E   34. _ ILL _ N _

35. F _ IE _ _ SH _ P   36. _ R _ V _   37. D _ _ ZLE

38. T _ AN _ FO _ _ T _ VE   39. _ RU _ T

40. SP _ _ KL _ NG POS _ T _ VE ATTIT _ D _

ANSWERS: 1.Love 2.Alive 3.Hug 4.Divine 5.Zing 6.Bubbly 7.Motivate 8.Manifest 9.Wonderful 10.Manifest 11.Bright 12.Shine 13.Energy 14.Effervescent 15.Peace 16.Awesome 17.Enthusiastic 18.Healing 19.Believe 20.Courageous 21.Vibrant 22.Delight 23.Exquisite 24.Relax 25.Marvellous 26.Thriving 27.Calm 28.Laughter 29.Visualisation 30.Encourage 31.Amazing 32.Harmony 33.Gratitude 34.Willing 35.Friendship 36.Brave 37.Dazzle 38.Transformative 39.Trust 40.Sparkling Positive Attitude

Did you do the exercise? What did this bring up for you?

Journal about your emotions that came up for you today, how good did it FEEL to shout out positive words? If you had others join in, how did that FEEL? Describe and FEEL into the joy that happened for you today ...

POSITIVE WORDS RULE

AMAZING • BEAUTIFUL • GENEROUS • GRATITUDE • kind • AMAZING • magic • ZING • PEACE • FAITH • DIVINE • COURAGE • vibrant • BELIEVE • FLOW • joy • AWESOME • tranquil • empower • ENERGY • CREATIVE • SPARKLE • LOVE • GLOW • calm • wow • FUN • BRAVE

NOTES

NOTES

DAY 8
RESISTING THE EGO
POSITIVITY PANTS

'Food for the ego is poison for the soul'
- Donna Goddard -

Whoop whoop! You are eight days into putting on your positive pants, I hope you are feeling pretty awesome and all your good thoughts are starting to feel aligned.

STOP for second ... breathe ...
... and answer the following question ...

Am I getting up every morning with a grateful heart? Remember to FEEL into the question (what does this bring up for you?)

_____

_____

_____

If you're new to this way of thinking it may take you a while to get into a routine, which is fine, don't worry yourself and most definitely DO NOT GIVE UP. That's why I devised this journal; **21 days of putting on your positivity pants, and NOT '1 week of putting on your positivity pants'!**

And remember, this is only a kick-start; you must CHOOSE to get up every morning and put them on even when you have finished this journal.

(Don't forget to join the 'Positive Pants Prints FB Group' to be updated on new journals, print & 'inspiring stuff!')

Hopefully, yesterday's exercise of shouting out random positive words helped to keep your vibes high. This is something you should try to do daily. It will especially help as we move onto the next part of this book, which is **'resisting our ego'**.

Today, we are talking about that little voice in our heads; the little voice, that appears on a morning, which can automatically send you into 'mood-hoover' mode. It sounds something like this ...

'I don't want to get up!', 'I'm SO tired!', 'I've got so much to do today: I can't function', 'I've got to deal with that miserable colleague at work today', 'It's three weeks until payday' !?!?

The little voice can often appear throughout the day and when we go to bed. Does this sound familiar?

'I can't do that: I'm not good enough!', 'I'll never be successful at that!', 'I'm not pretty enough, or skinny enough, or 'whatever' enough!', 'There's no point in me trying as something always goes wrong' !?!?

AND MY FAVOURITES, because I use to say them all the time, (Now, I want to shake (or hug) people when they say them)

'Knowing my luck ...'

'It could only happen to me ...'

MEET THE EGO; the ego is that little voice that discourages you because it comes from a place of fear.

Ok, this may sound like a negative journaling exercise but it's important to recognise our thoughts, yes, even the negative ones, because it allows us to identify them and change them ...

So, what did the above bring up for you?

_____

_____

_____

_____

_____

_____

_____

_____

_____

_____

_____

_____

_____

_____

In my younger days, my little voice would tell me I wasn't good enough, or worthy enough and obviously my favourite sayings **'Knowing my luck ...' or 'It could only happen to me ...'** were imbedded in my mind! *Cringe again*

Once I started to practice the Law of Attraction, (as you know, becoming slightly obsessed and qualifying in the subject) I realised, I was attracting the bad luck to me.

It gets to be fun when you start to practice positive words and ignore the ego!

If I use the above phrases now, it's because I believe I attract good luck, **i.e. knowing my luck, I'll win that prize.**

It's fun: you should try it!

Using good positive thoughts finish the sentences below 'knowing my luck' here ... (you don't have to fill them all in today, but come back to this page if things crop up for you in the future)

Knowing my luck _____ eg: *I will get the job!*

Knowing my luck _____

Knowing my luck _____

Knowing my luck _____

Knowing my luck _____

Knowing my luck _____

Knowing my luck _____

Knowing my luck _____

Knowing my luck _____

Now, don't get me wrong, I understand many things can affect our days, but if you focus on those issues, those issues become bigger. Think about this ... does it resonate with you?

If so, write your feelings about it here ...

_____
_____
_____
_____
_____
_____

Now, ask yourself, what thoughts can you change about this? How much are you listening to your ego? What are you learning from this situation?

_____
_____
_____
_____
_____
_____

When you come from a place of love and spirit, your soul nourishes good thoughts.

The ego is driving the doubt and negativity. The ego thrives off misery and worry. We often don't notice the damage the ego is doing. We simply accept that this is the way we feel.

It can stop us from having the fun-filled life we deserve. It's the ego that puts the doubt in our minds and makes us question our abilities.

The ego also wants to keep us safe! Not allowing us to venture out of our comfort zone, not allowing us to spread our wings, incase we fall! Fear drives the ego, resisting this will allow you to sore!

Do you recognise this voice?

_____
_____
_____
_____
_____

> "Only the ego resists egos.
> The spirit may notice egos,
> but sees beyond them and
> does not engage with them'
> - Alan Cohen -

Read the above quote again ... take it in and truly think about it!

Now, with that quote in mind, concentrate on the concept below ...

> We are souls in human bodies, having a human experience. Try to understand that there is something bigger at play. Come from a place of love and understanding. Once you're at that place you'll not even notice the ego. You will be guided by spirit and purpose.

What does this bring up for you?

_____
_____
_____
_____
_____
_____

Here's a few more questions for you to think about ...

What would you do with your life if the little voice in your head encouraged you, rather than discouraged you?

_____
_____
_____
_____

What would you do if you knew you couldn't fail?

_____
_____
_____
_____

What can you do today to make this happen?

_____
_____
_____
_____

You deserve to have the best life possible. So come from a place of love, spread your wings and fly!

Tell yourself today & everyday, **I FEEL AWESOME**.

The world is at your feet, choose love, choose passion, and choose to make a difference.

Tune into the little voice that wants the best for you.

Imagine your mind is a seed that needs feeding ... nurture it with loving thoughts and then listen to the goodness that grows, just as a blooming plant that is watered & taken care of.

YOU'VE GOT THIS!

NOTES

NOTES

DAY 9
LOVING & BELIEVING
IN MYSELF
POSITIVITY PANTS

'Believe in love. Believe in magic.
Hell, believe in Santa Clause.
Believe in others.
Believe in yourself.
Believe in your dreams.
If you don't, who will?
- Jon Bon Jovi -

To believe in yourself, you have to be fully aware of your consciousness and not listen to any doubts. Similar to yesterday, when we talked about ignoring that little negative voice. Resisting the ego.

People who have faith in their ability are the ones who are making a difference in the world. This doesn't mean they haven't doubted themselves, but they refuse to let that little voice influence them.

Many people are unhappy because they haven't followed their passion. Tomorrow we'll talk more about passion and inner guidance, but today, we will focus on you loving yourself and knowing you have the inner belief to make it happen.

How does the subject of loving yourself make you FEEL?

_____

_____

_____

_____

Many years ago, I would never have told people, 'I love myself'. Not only did I think it sounded egotistical, (there's that ego interfering again,) I also grew up in an environment where you could never think so highly of yourself. So I didn't!

Whereas now, I'm proud to say, 'I love myself'. I love who I am. I love that I come from a place of love; that I ONLY come from a place of love.

I don't think I'm better than anyone else, but also, I don't think anyone is better than me.

We are all as one and with our own little mission to make the world a better place ... once we come from this place, we get to see the world from a different perspective.

We start to understand it's not just about us. It's about 'serving' which is 'helping' ... all of this is done with love for ourselves & for others.

> *Love yourself. Respect yourself. Never sell yourself short. Believe in yourself regardless of what other people think.*
> *You can accomplish anything, absolutely anything, if you set your mind to it.'*
> *- Marcus Allen -*

Now let's digress a little (but hopefully you'll see a few of my points ... yes, there's a few!) before I became published, I was adamant I wanted to be a writer, I didn't care how it happened .. I wanted it SO bad! So before I was published by Bombshell Books I self-published.

Now, there's still a stigma when it comes to self-publishing ... however, there are plenty of amazing, bestselling authors out there, who have not let their fears hold them back.

If you believe that all self-publishers have been rejected, you are wrong. Some authors have never submitted to an agent or publisher, they have ignored their fears, taken their dream and ran with it.

Some authors have been accepted by agents and publishers and decided to become an indie author.

What points am I making?

- Don't let your judgements or the judgement of others stop you!
- Definitely don't let your ego stop you!
- If something is constantly calling to you, then it's meant for you!
- Acknowledge your fears, face them and do it anyway!

Do any other points come up for you?

_____
_____
_____
_____

Let's address the last point I made (acknowledging your fears) as this is super important because it is one of the things that holds many people back. So, trust me, when I say, being an author is one of the best ways to face your fears. It's one of the industries where work is openly criticised.

Any writer will tell you, their work is personal to them. So it's hard not to take a 1-star review personally. Especially, when readers can leave their reviews for the world to see.

Even J.K Rowling has had 1-star reviews. Can you imagine if J.K Rowling had decided not to write because she was scared someone would criticise her work? Can you imagine if she gave up after she was rejected 12 times from agents? Can you imagine if she'd focused on that?

The above relates to writing, but analysis this around your own dreams and goals. Research some people who have been successful in the area you are passionate about. What struggles did they have? What would have happened if they had not followed their dreams?

Sit with this, are you lacking in some kind of belief? Think about the people you admire, how do you relate to them? Imagine if they hadn't listened to their heart and soul? Bring your awareness to this FEELING and write about it here ...

_____
_____
_____
_____
_____
_____
_____
_____
_____
_____

So, ask yourself, while thinking of your idols, what's your big dream?

_____

_____

_____

_____

Imagine this dream is happening? How would you FEEL?

_____

_____

_____

_____

My aim is to spread as much encouragement to as many people as possible. I've been that person who didn't believe in myself, and trust me it took years to find that belief.

I realised once we come from a place of love, anything is possible, because we release all judgement, even from ourselves.

And when others judge, we realise that their judgement is about them, not us and we send them love!

I grew up thinking I wasn't anything special, but I felt a connection to something bigger than myself, but I was shot down if I did question it.

WE ARE ALL SPECIAL
REMEMBER THAT!

These days, I have my own beliefs in a higher power because I've used these techniques and it works. I know the Universe, and my loving angels, are looking after me; I know, they have got my back.

Just imagine for one second this is true for you too, (because I believe it is, I believe it's true for everyone).

I ask you to put good loving thoughts out there, **believe and love yourself**, so you can make wonderful things happen.

Don't listen to the voice that will hold you back, because this is simply fear asking you - what happens if I fail?

In the words of Erin Hanson:

> 'What happens if I fall?
> Oh, but my Darling,
> what happens if you fly?

When you've got the passion and determination, the Universe can't help but encourage you along, because you are projecting good thoughts and great vibes.

Follow the path that makes you tick, makes you want to jump out of bed on a morning, makes you want to shout from the rooftops, sends excitement through your soul and lifts your spirit high.

Believe in yourself and watch miracles happen. Know that you have got this and the Universe will deliver.

THE UNIVERSE LOVES YOU

Read these affirmations at least ten times throughout the day:

* I believe in me.

* I can do anything I want to do.

* I have a passion that will make me happy.

* I am determined to succeed in my chosen goals.

* I am beautiful. I am light. I am love.

* I believe in me.

NOTES

DAY 10
NO GUILT &
BIG BOUNDARY
POSITIVITY PANTS

'Givers need to set limits because takers rarely do.'
Rachel Wolchin

> *'Daring to set boundaries is about having the courage to love ourselves even when we risk disappointing others.'*
> *- Brene Brown -*

- Sometimes we say, 'yes' or 'no' to things to suit other people because we feel guilty.
- Sometimes we say, 'yes' or 'no' to things when we want to say the opposite.
- Sometimes we say, 'yes' or 'no' to things because we feel we have no choice.
- Sometimes we say, 'yes' or 'no' to things and it leaves us frustrated, dismayed and tired.

If you've experienced any of the above, it's time to pull on those no-guilt pants, put boundaries in place and do what is best for you.

How does the above resonate with you?

_____
_____
_____
_____

Putting our own needs first is something we don't often do. But to lead a happier life sometimes we have to put on those no-guilt positive pants and give ourselves some loving. You'll hopefully see by now, that gratitude, sending love, not judging yourself or others will make you feel lighter.

Are you feeling lighter? If so, write about how this FEELS. If not, ask yourself what can you do to FEEL lighter?

_____
_____
_____
_____

By doing what is best for you, doesn't mean you are no longer sending that love, you are giving it to yourself.

**Your own pot of love needs to be full,
so that you can give to others.**

Once you start chipping away at your own self-love, it chips away at any love you can give to others, whether you realise this or not.

Today, do two things …

1. Do something for yourself that you wouldn't usually do because you'd feel guilty, such as, have a bath during the day or book an appointment for a massage; something you would love to do but wouldn't dream of doing … get those no-guilt pants on & give yourself some loving.

How easy is it for you to do the above?

_____
_____
_____
_____

2. Think about things you have said, 'Yes' or 'No' to but wanted to say the opposite. Think of a scenario and replay it in your head.

What would have happened if you'd said, 'No' instead of 'Yes', or vice versa, what would have been the outcome? Imagine the good feelings that would come with that. Don't think about the negative implications (ie. the upsetting of someone etc.) think about the LOVE you would be giving to YOU! How good does that FEEL?

_____
_____
_____
_____

Is there something happening in the future that you wish you could say 'yes' or 'no' to? Write about this here and write about how good it will FEEL to do what YOU want to do ...

_____
_____
_____
_____
_____
_____
_____
_____
_____
_____
_____
_____
_____
_____
_____
_____
_____
_____
_____
_____
_____
_____
_____
_____

From now on, whenever you feel you SHOULD say 'Yes', but you WANT to say 'No', put on those no-guilt pants and do what is right for YOU! Boundaries are important for your own self love & care.

NOTES

DAY 11
I DESERVE TO BE WEARING POSITIVITY PANTS

You, yourself, as much as anybody in the entire universe, deserve your love and affection.'
- Buddha -

Over the last couple of days, we've talked about how many people don't follow their passion or their dreams because it would seem egotistical, or most people often play it safe because that's what they have been taught to do.

I grew up in an environment, where comments were made, such as; 'You'll never make it as an author', 'You're not strong enough to be a journalist, it's very competitive', and one of the best … 'It doesn't matter if you go to university, the man is the breadwinner and women stop at home to look after babies …'

Oh yes, I can feel a few people seething reading this.

But DON'T … go back to Day 3 and get those non-judgy pants on. It was a different time, a different era and luckily I knew there was more to life!

Does the above bring up anything for you?

I didn't listen to these comments. I refused to believe such old-fashioned restricted and limiting views. So I went on to university, completed a BA (HONS) in Business and Marketing, and I also became an author.

I didn't follow the journalism route, and if I was truthful, this was because of my own self-doubt and believing I wasn't good enough. However, I turned this around in my early thirties and went back to university and gained an MA in Creative Writing.

This is why I'm so passionate about positive pants wearing; I discovered we can be, and we can do, anything we want to, once we put our minds to it and believe in ourselves.

We deserve to believe and love ourselves. We deserve a wonderful life. YOU deserve a wonderful life.

> 'We are all of us stars,
> and we deserve to twinkle'
> - Marilyn Monroe -

I know you will find it much more fulfilling to focus on the good and know that you deserve to have a fantastic life. Don't look for things going wrong, get up each morning and tell yourself you deserve the best life.

You deserve to be wearing positivity pants every single day!

How does this make you FEEL?

_____
_____
_____
_____

Today, sit in a quiet place, where you can't be disturbed for ten minutes. Take in the silence and breathe in and out slowly.

Imagine you are surrounded by pure white light, imagine this white light is filled with love. This love is so powerful; you feel its warmth, security and trust.

You can't question if this love is real, because it is. It simply is.

Stay there longer than ten minutes if you can't feel it. Keep practising feeling this love as many times as you can in a day. You are so worthy of this love.

When you've done this, write about how it felt during & after?

_____
_____
_____
_____

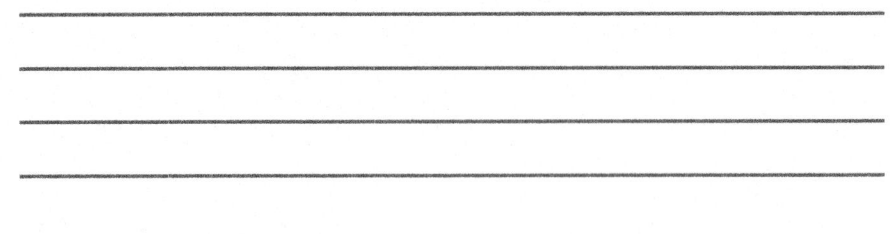

This love is the Universe's way of showing you that you deserve happiness. You deserve to jump out of bed and shout;

'I'M PUTTING ON MY POSITIVE PANTS!

I'VE SO GOT THIS!

I SO DESERVE THIS!'

'You deserve peace, love, happiness and
all that your heart desires.
Don't let anyone control your life
and take away those things'
- Sonya Parker -

NOTES

DAY 12
PURPOSE WITH PASSION
POSITIVITY PANTS

'If you can't figure out your purpose, figure out your passion. For your passion will lead you right into your purpose'
- Bishop T.D. Jakes- -

I get very excited when I talk about passion because I simply love it when people are following theirs. When a passion is being followed, there is something that lights up within a person.

Once you realise you deserve the best life and you are shouting about putting on your positive pants, it will surely help you follow your passion.

Do you FEEL as if you are following your passion?
If so, write about the LOVE you FEEL with this.
If not, what can you do to put steps in place to start following your passion?
Think about this and encompass the previous days of putting on your positive pants.
Remember you deserve to FEEL happy.
You deserve to FEEL love. YOU DESERVE TO BELIEVE IN YOURSELF AND MAKE THESE DREAMS COME TRUE!

Many people ask questions, such as, 'Why are we here?', 'What is the meaning of life?', 'What is our purpose?'

Let's get deep for a moment ...

Imagine you've had many past lives (whether you believe in them or not, try to imagine), imagine that in each lifetime we come back with the intention of learning more about our souls than our physical form. Imagine that we are here to learn about love and spirit. We are here to come from a place of love and to serve.

Sit with this for a moment, was does this bring up for you?

_____

_____

_____

_____

When you focus on this, when you dig deep and look at the reason you FEEL you are here, do you get excited?

Do you FEEL as if a boost of energy is flowing through you?

Today, take 10 minutes (or more) to breathe in this feeling, focus on what makes you tick, what lights you up inside?

Ask yourself; What excites me? What do I love doing? What fills me with pure love, joy and happiness?

Use the lines below and the next page to free write how this makes you FEEL?
Let go , let your thoughts be and let the pen flow ...

_____

_____

_____

_____

_____

'Passion is energy.
Feel the power that comes from
focusing on what excites you'
- Oprah Winfrey -

Remember: Small steps count!

Putting something, even the tiniest thing, in place daily will encourage you to keep moving towards those goals.

You'll be amazed at how adding something to your day that excites you, can lift your mood, which in turn will lift your vibrations and the way the Law of Attraction works, will bring good things to you.

If you are struggling to make your passions and purpose your priority, re-read the loving and believing in yourself positive pants and re-read the deserving positive pants.

If need be, re-read all the positive pants again and keep working on building that love for yourself.

IF YOU ARE READING THIS FAR, BE PROUD OF YOURSELF!

YOU HAVE TOTALLY GOT THIS!

NOTES

NOTES

DAY 13
VISUALISATION & IMAGINATION POSITIVITY PANTS

'Your imagination is your preview to life's coming attractions'
- Albert Einstein -

Remember when you were a child and you used your imagination to be anything, or anyone, you wanted to be. You believed in magic and miracles.

Can you remember the feeling of happiness when you were in these imaginary roles? Not a care in the world? Happiness galore? Freedom?

Take 5/10 minutes to think about role-playing when you were a child. If you have children of your own or within your family, watch how they flourish when in their own imaginary world.

What does this bring up for you?
_____
_____
_____
_____

The use of our imagination, is a powerful emotion that we lose as we get older and we start to analyse situations etc.

We listen to the rules that have been put in place by society. Rules that leave us feeling restricted.

We end up asking ourselves; is it wrong to want to live a wonderful and fulfilling life?

And you know my answer is ... absolutely not!

When we let go of 'what we should be doing', 'what is expected of us by society', infact, not even society, 'family and friends' can add that pressure too, but when we let go of this and come from a place of love, passion, purpose, fulfillment for ourselves, this extends outwards.

When your own wants are fulfilled, you become happier and this will have a ripple effect on the world around you.

You will hopefully be starting to see how your inner peace attracts the external pieces!

'Creative visualisation is a spiritual exercise using your thoughts and imagination to change your life in a positive way.'
- Meryl Hershey Beck -

So let's play a little game:

Imagine you are living the life you desire ... what would it look like? What would stay the same? What would change?

_____
_____
_____
_____
_____
_____
_____
_____
_____

Remember on day one, we talked about 'gratitude positivity pants' ... what can you be grateful for that you already have in your real life and your imagined life? What doesn't change?

_____
_____
_____
_____
_____
_____
_____
_____
_____

Imagination is one of the things that can lead to your reality.

Imagination can play a huge part in visualising your dreams.

Imagine the life you want to live. Imagine the life you deserve. And remember, you deserve a fantastic life. Be grateful for the things you've already bought into your life.

To help with using your imagination, a vision board is a great way to start.

A vision board can feature anything that you would love to have in your life; your dream car, your dream house, your dream relationship: find things in magazines and on the internet ... you can have so much fun with this, BUT it is about FEELING into it.

You can see the 'Vision Board Kit' with downloadables images and a mini video that will help you get the most out of your vision board (a link to teachable is at the front of the journal).

Many celebrities have created vision boards; Michelle Obama, Jim Carrey, Ellen DeGeneres and many more ...

> 'Whether you look at it from a spiritual or scientific aspect, this world is a huge vision board. Everything that's here is because it started as an image someone had in their mind. You want to call it a blueprint, or a business plan? Fine. But first, they had to think about it and draft it. So a vision board? It's like selling our own ideas to ourselves.'
> - Lucinda Cross -

Today, think about creating your own vision board.

If you can start on it, fantastic! It doesn't need to cost much. If you create a digital board, it doesn't have to cost you a penny!

Search for images on the Internet, start a Pinterest account and collect pictures of your dream life.

Simply have fun doing this, but remember to feel gratitude for these things. Appreciation will bring things to you much quicker.

Plus, FEEL into the FEELING!!!

Use this cloud to jot down some of the things you'd like to put on your vision board, use words also to help you FEEL into the FEELING!

NOTES

NOTES

DAY 14
MAGIC
POSITIVITY PANTS

'We do not need magic to change the world. We carry all the power we need inside ourselves already. We have the power to imagine better.'
- J.K.Rowling -

Believing in magic sounds like child's-play. But, ask yourself, how happy is the child who does believe in magic? Think back to yesterday's imagination positive pants!

Throughout these positive pants days you will have, hopefully, noticed a shift in your mood.

If you've been putting these pants on daily, nothing should faze you. You will automatically feel lighter.

**Feeling lighter will attract good things to you:
it will attract magical things to you.**

> 'The universe is almost like a huge magic trick and scientists are trying to figure out how it does what it does.'
> - Martin Gardener -

Do you go through life thinking, 'I'll believe it when I see it,' rather than, 'I'll see it when I believe it'?

So let's say that again: 'I'll see it when I believe it.' Close your eyes and think about that sentence.

What does this bring up for you? Do you need to work on your beliefs?

_____
_____
_____
_____
_____
_____
_____

The universe works in magical & mysterious ways. Believe the magic will happen and watch it unfold.

Magical things do happen; people fight cancer without treatment, people win the lottery, people have died and come back to life.

Some things happen in life that has us thinking, 'WOW! How did that happen?'

Real-life stories have us asking questions and seeking answers to something that is much bigger than us. Magical miracle moments can have us searching for a deeper meaning to life.

There will also be moments when we feel as if we can't take no more, but we grab onto something that turns our life around and we say things, such as, 'It's happening for a reason.'

That particular moment may not feel magical at the time, but if you think about the situation clearly, ask yourself, 'What did I learn?' 'What did I gain?' 'How has my life improved?'

Get those positive pants on and understand even at the darkest times, magic is happening. You just have to believe. I realise this is easier said than done, but sit with it and imagine where you could be if you BELIEVE IN MAGIC!

Write about this FEELING? The FEELING of being in such a magical place that it all FEELS aligned and comes together ...

When we identify with our soul and spirit, it can help us realise we are all here with the power to make miracles happen.

Today, your task is to research real-life magical miracle stories; read stories about people who have manifested their perfect relationship, people whose dreams have come true and people who have survived above all the odds.

Write some of your research here ... even use another notebook to start collecting these magical stories to help your belief grow.

Tune into your own magic today:
What magical things do you want to happen in your life?
Use your vision board, feel the feeling and put good high vibes out to the universe. Remember, to believe it and then you'll see it!

'The world is full of magic things,
patiently waiting for our senses
to grow sharper'
- W.B Yeats -

NOTES

NOTES

DAY 15
POSITIVE
PLANNING
PANTS

'Let our advance worrying become our advance thinking and planning.'
- Winston Churchill -

The last two days we talked about vision boards and making the magic happen. Over the past two weeks we have talked about different types of positive pants; this collection of positive pants should help you feel gratitude while still focusing on your dreams.

This journal is designed to help you focus on things you love, the things you would love to have in your life, the things you deserve, the things you are grateful for etc.

So on Day 15, we are looking at bringing these past two weeks together with a positive pants plan!

Once you have a focus, an aim and you're not just muddling through life, day by day unable to get off, what I call, 'the treadmill of life', you will feel happier.

If something makes you happy, do it!

If you can't do it today, what can you do to make it happen? What plans can you put in place to make sure you can live the life you want?

Do you need to do more studying? Training? Mindfulness?

REMEMBER, SMALL STEPS COUNT!

Whatever plans you put in place, make sure they fit with your life. If you are putting too much pressure on yourself your plans will fall apart, this will stress you out further and is not the way forward for positive pants wearing!

So make sure you PLAN around YOU!

'Planning is bringing the future into the present so that you can do something about it now'
- Alan Lakem -

Use the next few pages to jot down some ideas and then put some structure to these plans to help you move forward.

How can I make my ideas work ... what steps can I take?

THE IDEA

WHAT STEPS DO I NEED TO MAKE THIS HAPPEN?

WHAT TIMELINES CAN I EXPECT THESE THINGS TO HAPPEN?

**What other things do you need so you can
put these plans in place?
Use this page to jot down anything that comes to mind ...**

**Now, imagine these plans were taking place, this was happening ... YOU ARE MAKING THIS HAPPEN ...
HOW DOES THAT FEEL?**

_____
_____
_____
_____
_____
_____
_____
_____
_____
_____
_____
_____

*'Have a bias towards action -
let's see something happen now.
You can break that big plan into small steps
and take the first step right away'
- Indira Gandhi -*

Small steps and little plans will help you work towards your goal.

If you achieve more in a particular day, then get those awesome high-five pants on.

Plan it, visualise it, manifest it ... you got this!

If you don't know
where you are going,
you'll end up
someplace else
- Yogi Berra -

NOTES

DAY 16
POSITIVELY
GOOD MOOD
PANTS

'The most important decision you will ever make is to be in a good mood'
- Voltaire -

Over two weeks of putting on your positivity pants, and with yesterday's positive planning, you should be feeling lighter and brighter ... are you excited?

Have you noticed that the lighter and brighter you feel, the world seems a lighter and brighter place?

_____
_____
_____

Have you been able to let things go that would usually bother you? Have you released all judgements, angst and sent out lots of love?

_____
_____
_____

The Law of Attraction works on feelings and emotions. The universe responds to your feelings.

Have you noticed if you start the day in a bad mood, it seemingly gets worse? If you jump out of bed with those positivity pants on, you'll find good things happening throughout the day. (It could be simple things, such as someone let you jump the queue in the shop, or it could be something more significant, such as you won a contract at work.) **Does this resonate with you?**

_____
_____
_____
_____
_____
_____

Even the smallest wins should be appreciated. Saying thank you and truly appreciating the small and big wins, will put you in a good mood.

A good mood will bring you good things. This is a great quote from Abraham Hicks, that reiterates all that you've been doing over the last two weeks:

> '... do everything and anything you can to keep yourself in a good mood; use your physical senses. There is such beauty to be seen with your eyes. And there is such beauty to be heard with your ears. There is such beauty to be smelled with your nose. And experienced with your sensual body. And there is beauty to be experienced with your taste. Experience the beauty and feel the resonance of source'

Sometimes, the best thing to do is sit, take a breath and take in the world. See it, hear it, smell it, taste it ... so that you can FEEL it.

Today, get those good mood pants on by taking in the beauty around you; visit the beach or take a walk in the hills, and breathe in our wonderful world.

If you don't have the opportunity to experience the beach or the hills, take a step outside; visit your local park, or simply step out of your house. There is so much beauty around us that we take for granted.

Research has shown that being outside can boost our oxygen levels, and this will boost our serotonin levels, which leads to feelings of happiness and relaxation. So a simple 5-minute walk could have you feeling amazing.

Write about what you noticed when you did this exercise ... use all your senses to FEEL into this ... what did you see? Hear? Smell? etc.

_____
_____
_____
_____
_____
_____
_____
_____
_____
_____
_____
_____

How does the above make you FEEL?

_____
_____
_____
_____
_____
_____
_____
_____
_____
_____
_____
_____

What wonderful things have made you smile today ... hopefully the colour of the trees, the breeze on your face or the friendly acknowledgement of a passer by?

Write about this and the gratitude you FEEL for it ...

'Today, you can choose to be in a good mood, or a bad mood. Give yourself permission to be happy every day'
- Joel Osteen -

life is like a
camera
focus on what's important
capture the
good times
and if things
don't work out
just take
another
shot

NOTES

NOTES

DAY 17
POSITIVE
LAUGHTER
PANTS

'I am thankful for laughter, except when milk comes out of my nose'
- Woody Allen -

I love today's laughing pants and I love the quote from Woody Allen ... maybe it's not great if milk comes out of your nose, but, let's face it, that type of laughter is the best!

Every day should include laughter.

I believe laughter is our souls speaking. The feeling when true laughter hits is amazing.

Throughout your positive pants days, have you been journaling about how thankful you are for laughter? Has anything hit home that has truly made you laugh?

_____
_____
_____
_____

You have more than likely heard the saying, 'Laughter is the best medicine', well, research has shown this is true.

There are so many physical and mental health benefits of laughing, it strengthens the immune system, it can diminish pain and it can protect the body from the negative effects of stress. Research has also shown that laughter brings people together and strengthens relationships.

On this positive pants journey you'll be discovering the lighter you feel, the more receptive you are to laughter. You will start to see the funnier side to life, rather than looking at life so seriously.

Does this resonate with you?

_____
_____
_____
_____
_____
_____

A little laughter can give you a huge boost ...

As a start, here are ten ways to increase laughter in your life, but because this is a journal, guess what, we are going to do some journaling around each one!

Instead of just reading, make a note about how you can bring each point into your life. Research if needed (i.e: favourable YouTube/comedians/sitcoms) as this will help you take action.

1. Watch YouTube: There are plenty of funny videos on YouTube. Videos of babies laughing, or funny pranks being caught on camera, are always a winner.

_____

_____

_____

2. Watch a comedian: Many people have a favourite comedian. If you search YouTube or Google, you will soon find some hilarious comedians.

_____

_____

_____

3. Watch a funny sitcom or TV programme: There are plenty of comedies and programmes that are very funny. The good thing about watching a sitcom is you get to know the characters as the weeks progress, this in turn, makes it more entertaining for the viewer, as they understand the characters personalities.

_____

_____

_____

'Earth laughs in flowers'
- Ralph Waldo Emerson -

4. Be around children: Children can make us laugh just by watching them play, listening to them chat, or asking them a question. Asking a child to describe something is a great way to lighten your mood.

_____
_____
_____

5. Write down any funnies: If something funny happens in your day, write it down or, if a child says something funny, write it down … keep these for the future, if you need a pick-me-up.

_____
_____
_____

6. Think about a funny story: There will be times in your life, when something has happened that is very funny. Re-tell the story to yourself and others.

_____
_____
_____

7. Attract funny people: We've talked lots about the Law of Attraction; what you put out there you are attracting back. Therefore, if you are spending your days laughing, you'll attract people into your life who are fun to be around.

_____
_____
_____

8. Read a funny book: There are plenty of funny books out there. Look through Amazon, search the humour books, there will be something that takes your fancy. 'Your vibe attracts your tribe.'

_____
_____
_____

9. Look in the mirror and pull faces: Believe it or not this actually works. It's even better if you do it with someone. So much fun to be had.

10. Fake it, until it's real: This works too. Smile and laugh to yourself. You'll soon find yourself laughing for real.

If you can't seem to find any laughter through any of the suggested ways, have a research on the internet and make it your mission to have a giggle. Make it your mission to laugh every day.

How hard have you found this? What can you do to bring more laughter into your life? Can you make it your mission to laugh every single day?

Once you have laughed until your sides are sore, remember to appreciate the moment.

LOVE LAUGH LIVE
LOVE LAUGH LIVE
LOVE LAUGH LIVE
LOVE LAUGH LIVE

a day
without
laughter
is a day
wasted

LOVE LAUGH LIVE
LOVE LAUGH LIVE
LOVE LAUGH LIVE
LOVE LAUGH LIVE

NOTES

NOTES

DAY 18
POSITIVE
PARTY
PANTS

'Start each day like
it's your birthday'
- Kate Spade -

One of my favourite books is by Kyle Gray, 'Raise Your Vibrations'.

On page 77 of this book, he talks about Vibe 19; Divine Dance Party. I love this. I love his idea about the angels dancing with him. Angels are a huge part of our lives, and once we acknowledge them, the friendship that we formed is unbreakable. When you know angels support you, you can ask them questions, and you'll be surprised how they answer. Just simply, look for the signs.

Imagine jumping out of bed every day with your positive party pants on, as if, in the words of Kate Spade, it's your birthday.

How does the above make you FEEL? Can you imagine jumping from your bed in this way?

_____

_____

_____

_____

_____

I'll reiterate: The Law of Attraction is always working, if you are sending out high vibrations, you will receive high vibe energy back.

So if you were to put on those positive pants every day and feel as if life is a party, can you imagine the vibrations that you would be giving off?

You would be smoking: positive steam would be releasing from every pore, the universe would have no option but to bring you more positive party pants to wear.

Today, take some time to put on some music and have a dance. If you have other family members with you, get them to join in.

You'll be surprised how 5 minutes of listening to playful tunes can lift your mood. Try and imagine the angels surrounding you and give them a high-five … this is one of my favourite things to do: high-fiving the angels. You must try it.

Did you do this today? How did it FEEL? Writing down how it felt will help you connect and bring more of that feeling to you.

_____

_____

_____

_____

_____

Music is a great way to get those positive pants on. An upbeat tune, a little twist and shake around the room and angel high-fiving is an extremely great way to start your day.

Your vibrations will be lifted and you will be emitting positive pants wearing to the Universe, and this will only give you more reasons to keep putting on those positive pants because the universe will reflect these vibes back to you.

Today, reflect for 10 minutes on one of your best birthdays you've ever had. If you can't think of a good birthday, think about a good time in your life, a day that felt amazing ...

Write about why this was the best birthday, or the best time in your life ... how did it make you FEEL?

_____

_____

_____

_____

_____

_____

_____

_____

_____

Take that feeling throughout your days with you.

NOTES

NOTES

DAY 19
POSITIVELY
EMBRACING LIFE
PANTS

'Embrace uncertainty.
Some of the most beautiful
chapters in our lives
won't have a title
until much later'
- Bob Goff -

Hopefully, every day you are bouncing out of bed putting on your positive pants, but on a serious note, there could be things going on in your life that you wish you could change.

Maybe you are trying to focus on the good things but you're struggling ... why am I mentioning this so far into the book? Because as you've read through each pair of positive pants your mindset will be growing, expanding and developing.

> *'Challenges are what makes life interesting. Overcoming them is what makes life meaningful'*
> *- Joshua J. Marine -*

We talked about focusing on what you want, but it's important to understand that there will be things in our life that we want to improve or change.

Does this bring anything up for you? Write about how you've felt about embracing the positive pants journey ...

_____
_____
_____
_____
_____
_____
_____
_____
_____
_____

Sometimes, something happens out of our control, but how we respond to it can help us deal with something we are not happy about.

Sometimes the universe throws us a curveball because we deserve something better.

So maybe you've been made redundant or a relationship has ended, imagine an opportunity arising and being presented to you that is better than the situation you've come from.

How does this make you FEEL? Does this bring anything up for you?

_____
_____
_____
_____
_____

Encompass everything you've been learning over the positive pants journey and embrace it. Be grateful, send out good positive vibes and embrace any situation that you would like to improve. Look for the positive aspects. Ask yourself, 'What can I learn from this?'

Today, think about a situation you wish you could change & imagine something amazing coming out of the situation. Express your gratitude for this awesome outcome.

_____
_____
_____
_____
_____

Write some more about this ... use the visualisation, imagination and magical positive pants to bring together your thoughts about embracing your journey.

Let your thoughts be, FEEL into your FEELINGS and let your pen flow.

NOTES

DAY 20
POSITIVELY
TRUSTING YOUR JOURNEY
PANTS

'Your journey has molded you for the greater good. It was exactly what it needed to be.
Don't think you've lost time.
It took each and every situation you have encountered to bring you to the now.
And now, is right on time'
- Asha Tyson -

The fact you've come this far in the journal is awesome, give yourself a pat on the back. It shows you are committed to wearing positive pants only! No more negative knickers or boring boxers, absolutely not, you want a drawer full of positivity pants.
If you want it, you can do it!

So you've nearly finished your 21 days of getting up and putting on those positive pants. How are you FEELING?

_____

_____

_____

_____

_____

Hopefully, you've realised that good high vibes help to attract more high vibes into your life.

Hopefully, you are recognising that we are on this journey together. Obstacles, challenges or difficulties will arise, but if we ask ourselves, 'What will I learn from this situation?' It makes these barriers and rollercoaster moments easier to deal with.

Just as yesterday when we talked about embracing the journey. Try to relax and go with the flow. Trust that everything will work out for you if you trust the process.

> 'So trust the process of your life unfolding, and know with certainty, through the peaks and valleys of your journey, that your soul rests safe and secure in the arms of God'
> - Dan Millman -

So, we've put good vibes out to the universe, we've used the Law of Attraction, we've put on our positive pants daily and perhaps you feel you haven't received what you want, what you asked for or what you desire …

Does this sound familiar? It's so easy to become disheartened and allow our thoughts to spiral. We then start to feel frustrated. But imagine if the universe is delivering more than what you asked for.

Your vibes are so high the universe is giving you what you deserve … which is an abundance of happiness.

So keep those positive pants on, don't focus on the situations that may hold you back.

Focus on having a great journey, trust that everything that happens, happens for a reason. Sometimes it's a wake-up call, and sometimes it's a push in another direction … the right direction.

Your job is to trust that the universe has your back.

Trusting your journey here on this physical plane is meaningful; you have something to give to others, you are here to serve a purpose and most importantly come from a place of love. Once you can accept this, all the positive pants wearing we've been doing will become easier.

When you stop judging and complaining and come from a place of acceptance, things start to make sense.

Today, think about a past situation, that upset you at first but delivered a better outcome. Think about a situation that you expected something to happen but it didn't, you ended on another path that had better results.

There will be times in your life when it hasn't gone to plan, but look for the positives that came out of these situations. Use the following page to journal about this.

**Trust that everything has been mapped out for you.
Your job is to have fun and enjoy life's road-trip.
Accept it, relish in it and trust it.**

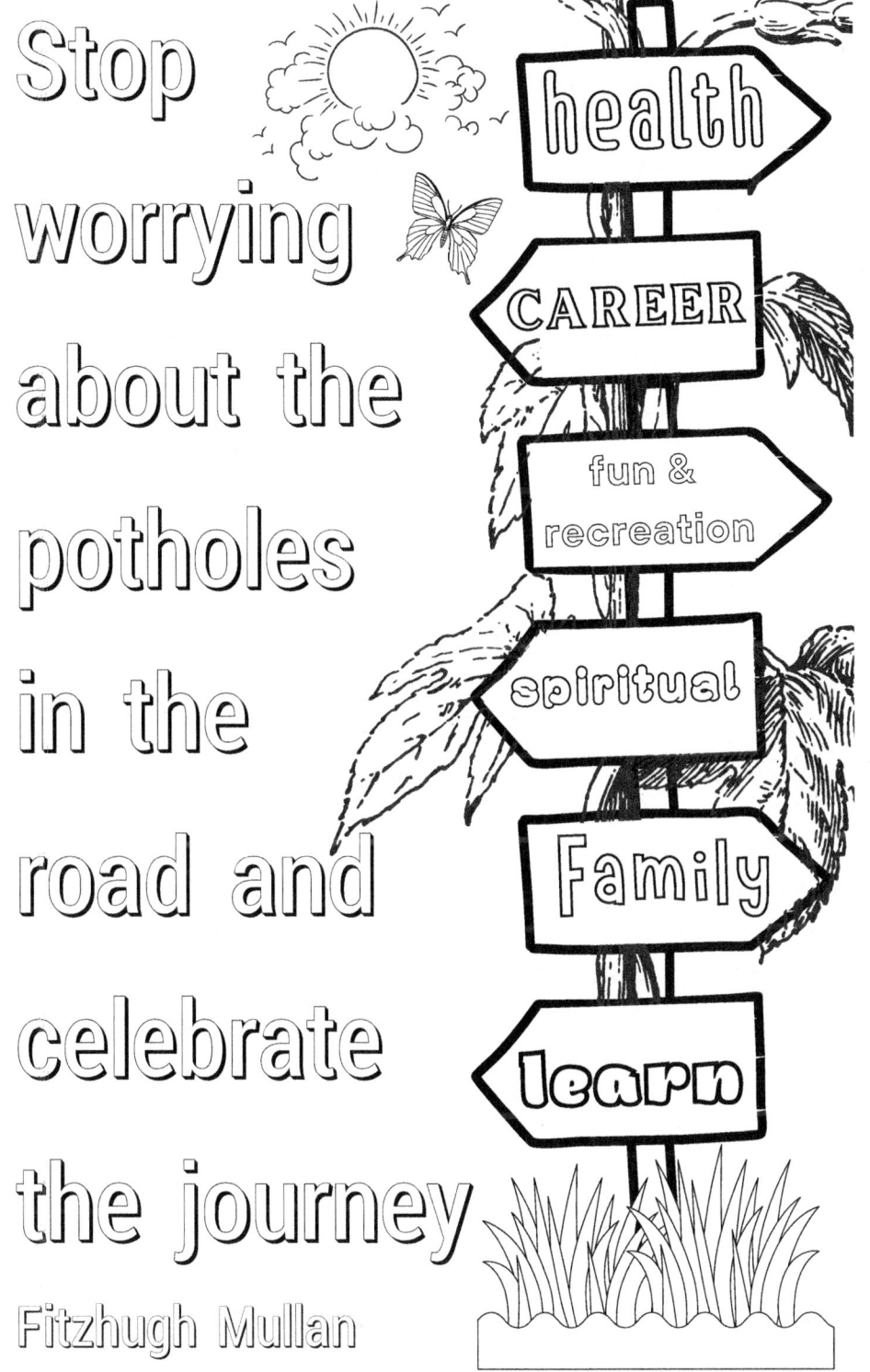

Stop worrying about the potholes in the road and celebrate the journey

Fitzhugh Mullan

NOTES

DAY 21
BIGGEST
BRIGHTEST
POSITIVE PANTS

'Let your light shine so brightly that others can see their way out of the dark'

- Katrina Mayer -

Well done you! 21 days of putting on your positive pants. Amazing work!

Let's have a high-five party: high-five those angels, shout some positive words, have a dance and be extremely proud of yourself.

21 days of learning strategies to become more open to good vibes. The challenge after this is to keep it going. Get up every morning with positive pants on only.

> *'I will put on my biggest brightest positive pants every single day. So I can attract the brightest life and spread that brightness to others'*

Surround yourself with positivity, remind yourself that you are in a good place and always look for something to smile about.

To finish off your last day of the positive pants journey, here are some affirmations, that you could do every morning to remind yourself you are pretty awesome.

Have a little journal about how you FEEL about each affirmation, use positive words only!

Brightness shines through me when I wear my positive pants

_____

_____

I always wear my biggest brightest positive pants

_____

_____

Gratitude illuminates from me when I'm wearing my positive pants

_____

_____

Great vibes surround me when I wear my positive pants

_____
_____

Every day starts with me putting on my biggest brightest positive pants

_____
_____

Singing feels so good when I put my positive pants on

_____
_____

The best days are those when I put my positive pants on

_____
_____

Believing it while wearing my positive pants helps me see it

_____
_____

Radiance pours from me when I wear my positive pants

_____
_____

I love and believe in myself when I wear my positive pants

_____
_____

Great things happen when I have my positivity pants on

_____
_____

Habits are easy to make or break when I have my positive pants on
_____
_____

Thinking terrific, powerful, amazing thoughts when my positive pants are on
_____
_____

Easiness flows through me when I have my positive pants on
_____
_____

Starting the day with a smile because I'm wearing my positivity pants
_____
_____

Trusting my journey while wearing my positive pants
_____
_____

Perfect days happen for me when I'm wearing my positive pants
_____
_____

Awesome, wonderful things happen when I put my positive pants on
_____
_____

No negative knickers in my drawer, positive pants only
_____
_____

True pure joy fills me when I put my positive pants on
_____
_____

Smiling my way through the day because I'm wearing my positive pants

_____

_____

Every day should start with something to smile about.

**Before you leave your bed,
your first thoughts should be gratitude.**

**Appreciating the day in front of you will help you
jump out of bed and put on your positive pants.**

**You've got this:
Smile, Be Joyful, and Be Happy.
Look for the brighter things in life,
fill your heart with gratitude and appreciate
where you are and look forward to more
wonderful things happening.**

You've got this

biggest brightest positive pants

NOTES

NOTES

NOTES

NOTES

NOTES

NOTES

NOTES

NOTES

NOTES

Printed in Great Britain
by Amazon